IMAGES OF V

ARMOURED WARFARE
FROM THE
RIVIERA TO THE RHINE
1944–1945

RARE PHOTOGRAPHS FROM WARTIME ARCHIVES

Anthony Tucker-Jones

Pen & Sword
MILITARY

First published in Great Britain in 2016 by
PEN & SWORD MILITARY
an imprint of
Pen & Sword Books Ltd,
47 Church Street,
Barnsley,
South Yorkshire
S70 2AS

A CIP record for this book is available from the British Library.

ISBN 978 1 47382 146 0

Typeset by CHIC GRAPHICS

Printed and bound by CPI Group (UK) Ltd, Croydon, CR0 4YY

Pen & Sword Books Ltd incorporates the imprints of Pen & Sword Archaeology,
Atlas, Aviation, Battleground, Discovery, Family History, History, Maritime, Military,
Naval, Politics, Railways, Select, Social History, Transport, True Crime, Claymore
Press, Frontline Books, Leo Cooper, Praetorian Press, Remember When, Seaforth
Publishing and Wharncliffe.

For a complete list of Pen & Sword titles please contact
Pen & Sword Books Limited
47 Church Street, Barnsley, South Yorkshire, S70 2AS, England
E-mail: enquiries@pen-and-sword.co.uk
Website: www.pen-and-sword.co.uk

Contents

Introduction

The armoured battles fought from the Riviera to the Rhine were characterised by a rapid advance by American and French armoured divisions until they reached the mountains on the Franco-German border. This was part of General Eisenhower's broad front strategy following the Allies' defeat at Arnhem. Remarkably, although General Johannes Blaskowitz's German Army Group G had lost most of its panzers to the fighting in Normandy, it was still able to keep the American and French armour at bay in southern France.

Unlike in Normandy, where there was a three-month deadlock following D-Day, the Operation Dragoon landings in the Riviera saw the Allies swiftly overcome the German defences. However, Blaskowitz conducted an exemplary fighting withdrawal, thanks to the actions of the 11th Panzer Division. It was not until the Battle of Arracourt and the creation of the Montélimar and Colmar pockets that the Germans suffered their first major defeats in southwest Europe, opening the way into Germany across the Rhine.

The British Prime Minister Winston Churchill announced the Liberation of France to the House of Commons on 28 September 1944:

> An American and French landing on the Riviera coast, actively assisted by a British airborne brigade, a British air force and the Royal Navy, has led with inconceivable rapidity to the capture of Toulon and Marseilles, to the freeing of the great strip of the Riviera coast, and to the successful advance of General Patch's army up the Rhône valley. This army, after taking over 80,000 prisoners, joined hands with General Eisenhower, and has passed under his command.

The plan had been to capitalise on the Allies' success in Normandy with an invasion of the Riviera in mid-1944, with the intention of trapping the Germans as they had done in the north. Churchill, the wily old politician, avoided the inconvenient truth that most of the German army in southern France had escaped the clutches of the Allies and was now offering a determined rearguard defence west of the Rhine.

In the south there was no hiding Adolf Hitler's inability to effectively hold the coast. General Blaskowitz's Army Group G, with its headquarters in Toulouse, had responsibility for General Kurt von der Chevallerie's 1st Army and General Friedrich Wiese's 19th Army stationed on the Biscay and Riviera coasts respectively, but his command was fatally weakened by the requirement to send a steady stream of reinforcements north to counter the D-Day landings. Those units from Army Group G sent to Normandy suffered around 40,000 killed or wounded, and none of the survivors was reassigned to Blaskowitz.

In early June 1944 Blaskowitz's command totalled fewer than twenty divisions but by mid-August it had been reduced to just seven: six infantry and one panzer, although four of the infantry units were not combat ready. Chevallerie was left with a single corps, while Wiese only had the 11th Panzer Division and some second-rate static infantry divisions. During the run-up to the Allied invasion of the Riviera Blaskowitz had about 30,000 troops facing the invasion beaches, although within a few days' march there were over 200,000.

Blaskowitz knew that time was of the essence; he could not hope to hold the Allies on the coast and would have to conduct a swift fighting withdrawal into the French interior. In the wake of American attempts to break out of the Normandy bridgehead, Colonel Horst Wilutzky, Blaskowitz's operations officer, attended a briefing at the headquarters of Field Marshal Günther von Kluge, CinC West, on 1 August 1944. Wilutzky and General von Gyldenfeldt, Blaskowitz's chief of staff, had concluded that 'there was no military justification for holding German units in southern France any longer', and Blaskowitz and Kluge agreed, but Hitler pointlessly insisted that Army Group G stay put for another two weeks, by which time it was almost too late.

Blaskowitz put his cards on the table and informed Kluge that because of the 'release of men and weapons [Army Group G's] defensive power has become considerably smaller and … a successful defence of the coast is no longer guaranteed'. On 8 August Kluge and his chief of staff, General Hans Speidel, decided it was imperative that Blaskowitz be saved. 'It's time to abandon the South of France,' Kluge urged. 'Why leave the 1st Army on the Atlantic now we know the outcome of the war is at stake. Let us put Army Group G on the line Seine–Loire–Gien–Nevers–Gex. Let's abandon Provence.' Despite his efforts, it would be another week before any withdrawal was given the green-light by Hitler.

By the summer of 1944, in the wake of the Allied landings on the French Riviera, Hitler's forces were in full flight from southern France. He watched in dismay as his defences in the region unravelled. To make matters worse, German resistance in Normandy was almost at an end. In the south the swift advance of General Jean de Lattre de Tassigny's French 1st Army and General Alexander Patch's US 7th Army caught Hitler by surprise. Leaving Toulon and Marseilles to the French forces, Patch's advance guard raced to reach the city of Grenoble on 22 August, with the objective of linking up with elements of General George Patton's US 3rd Army near Dijon.

The sole remaining escape route for Hitler's troops lay in the network of roads and rail lines in the 24km-wide Belfort Gap, between the Vosges mountains to the north and the Jura mountains to the southeast. Hitler dispatched the 11th Panzer Division to Besançon on the evening of 5 September to cover the retreating German 19th Army as it moved into Belfort. Hitler's high command also ordered the 30th Waffen-SS Division to France. This arrived in Strasbourg on 18 August with instructions to hold the Belfort Gap and counter any Free French units operating in the area.

Fighting in the freezing snows covering Alsace, the French army finally avenged its humiliating defeat of 1940. Supported by American forces, French troops first surrounded and then overwhelmed some eight enemy divisions, inflicting almost 40,000 casualties on the German 19th Army. This, though, was no daring Blitzkrieg; it was warfare at its worst with General Charles de Gaulle's vengeful French literally bludgeoning the Germans to death. General Joseph de Goislard de Monsabert's troops launched their attack in the winter of 1944/5 determined to destroy the last Nazi foothold on French soil.

For those German troops abandoned by Adolf Hitler west of the Rhine, a miserable fate awaited them. They had prepared their trenches, bunkers and minefields in the full knowledge that they would be far safer on the eastern bank of this mighty barrier. As ever, though, Hitler, even at this late stage of the war, would hear no talk of tactical or strategic withdrawals: his men must fight and die where they stood. Shivering in the bitter cold, wrapped in tatty greatcoats, their breath a misty vapour, they knew they were standing in the way of the Allies' southern thrust into the Nazi heartland. Now an army of frightened schoolboys and pensioners, with most of the veterans long gone, they lacked everything from bullets to food. This was no way to fight a war, but they had no choice; their families were depending on them.

The vast Nazi bridgehead on the west bank of the Rhine, some 65km long and 50km deep, was created when Hitler's defences in the Vosges mountains collapsed following the attack by the US 6th Army Group in late 1944. By this stage the reinvigorated French army consisted of highly experienced colonial troops who had fought their way up from the south of France and green recruits who had recently come from the Free French forces of the FFI (the French Army of the Interior, better known as the Resistance). This reorganisation, plus a lack of supporting arms, including artillery, meant that the French forces were weaker than the other Allied field armies. It was this that enabled Hitler to hold the Colmar Pocket against an unsuccessful French offensive that ran from 15 to 22 December 1944.

In January 1945, despite Hitler's Ardennes offensive running out of steam, he launched Operation North Wind in an effort to recapture Strasbourg. Participating were the 198th Infantry Division and the 106th Panzer Brigade attacking north from the Colmar Pocket from 7 to 13 January. Although the defending French 2nd Corps suffered some minor losses during this attack, they held south of Strasbourg and frustrated Hitler's attempts to grab the city.

Following the failure of *Nordwind*, the 6th Army Group was ordered to crush the Colmar Pocket as part of General Dwight D. Eisenhower's plan for all Allied forces to reach the Rhine prior to invading Nazi Germany. Since the bulk of Allied troops surrounding the pocket were French, the honour of destroying the German 19th Army was granted to the French 1st Army. In the meantime in the north all eyes were turned on Generals Montgomery and Patton as they vied to be the first to cross the Rhine.

Photograph Sources

The images in this book have been sourced via the author from various archives including the US Army and US Signal Corps, as well as his own considerable collection. Readers interested in the D-Day landings and the fighting in Normandy may like to consult the author's companion volumes, *Images of War: Armoured Warfare in the Battle for Normandy* and *Images of War: Armoured Warfare in Northwest Europe 1944–1945*, also published by Pen & Sword.

Chapter One

The Riviera Dilemma

Just over two months after the momentous D-Day landings in Normandy in June 1944, the 'other D-Day' took place in the south of France. The bitter arguing over the validity of this operation was such that it almost threatened to bring down the British government. General Dwight D. Eisenhower, the American Allied Supreme Commander, described the row with Britain's leader as 'one of the longest sustained arguments that I had with Prime Minister [Winston] Churchill throughout the period of the war'.

The Allied fight against the Axis forces had gathered momentum by 1944 following a series of successful actions, particularly Operation Torch, the Anglo-American landings against French North Africa in November 1942, Operation Husky and the capture of Sicily in July 1943 and the subsequent invasion of southern Italy in September 1943. That year the proposed invasion of southern France, initially dubbed Operation Anvil (then Dragoon), emerged to complement Operation Hammer, the attack on northern France (which later became Overlord). The idea was to divide the German defences in France and prevent their forces in the south moving north to oppose the cross-Channel assault.

The Soviet leader Joseph Stalin was also pressing for an attack on southern France; he wanted the western Allies distracted from the Balkans, so that the Red Army would have a free hand to punish Hitler's east European allies and secure Yugoslavia. It was Stalin who gained both Churchill's and President Roosevelt's commitment to Anvil at their Tehran Conference in 1943, although Churchill and the British chiefs of staff really wanted all military resources directed to opening a second front in Normandy and continuing the on-going campaign in Italy. In late February 1944 Eisenhower obtained agreement for continued planning for Anvil from the combined chiefs of staff and approval from Roosevelt and Churchill.

Churchill ultimately saw this operation as a waste of effort, needlessly drawing troops and equipment from Italy. There was also concern that German troops in Italy might strike westwards at the invasion force's eastern flank. The British argued that resources would be better allocated to the Allied troops in Italy, which would enable a decisive thrust up the Italian peninsula, through Austria and into southern Germany

– this would render both Anvil and even Overlord unnecessary. The Americans argued that both geography and logistics were against such a plan; crossing the English Channel meant shorter lines of communication and a line of advance that was not obstructed by the troublesome Alps.

To General Sir Henry Maitland Wilson, the British theatre commander in the Mediterranean, the American preoccupation with France's southern ports seemed 'to imply a strategy aimed at defeating Germany during the first half of 1945 at the cost of an opportunity of defeating her before the end of 1944'. Wilson warned the British chiefs of staff that a diversion of forces for Anvil would cause a pause in offensive operations in the Mediterranean of at least six months, allowing the Germans to establish themselves strongly in Italy along their defensive Pisa–Rimini Gothic Line.

Likewise, Hitler saw the Italian front as the key front; holding on there helped reduce Allied air attacks on his factories in central Europe and protected the vital raw materials of the Balkans. In contrast, for him southern France had no strategic importance whatsoever. A withdrawal from there would surrender nothing of strategic or economic value and would give the Allies no airbases nearer to his war industries than they already possessed. His U-boat bases on the Bay of Biscay were no longer of any great utility and the disruption of the French railways had already curtailed what raw materials he had obtained from France and Spain.

At the end of June General Wilson withdrew the bulk of the American units assigned to Anvil from the front lines in Italy, as well as four French divisions, but all were exhausted and in need of rest and recuperation. Churchill was conscious that the Allied forces in Italy had already lost seven divisions (four American and three British) which had been sent back to Britain for the cross-Channel assault, and the loss of a further seven for Anvil seemed the final straw. Churchill feared that by weakening the Allied forces in Italy further they would be unable to destroy the German armies there and reach Vienna, thereby countering Soviet influence in central Europe.

Churchill stepped up his campaign to derail Anvil and cabled President Roosevelt, pleading, 'Let's not wreck one great campaign for the sake of another. Both can be won.' But Roosevelt would not give in and on 29 June 1944 he cabled back: 'In view of the Soviet–British–American agreement, reached at Tehran, I cannot agree without Stalin's approval to the use of force or equipment elsewhere.' This, of course, was not strictly true, but it meant that Churchill was essentially whistling in the wind, although he refused to accept this to the last.

Throughout July 1944 Churchill bombarded Eisenhower with cables, driving the Allied Supreme Commander to distraction. Eisenhower recalled: 'This argument, beginning almost coincidentally with the break-through [in Normandy] in late July, lasted throughout the first ten days of August.' As late as the week before the Riviera landings Churchill sought to bully Eisenhower into getting his own way. Relations became particularly acrimonious when he pitched up at Eisenhower's Normandy HQ (codenamed Shellburst), near the village of Tournières, 12 miles southwest of Bayeux, on 7 August.

Churchill wanted Eisenhower to shift Anvil to Brittany or the Channel ports, which would have piled more pressure on the Germans in northern France, although in reality there was a lack of available ports as the Germans resolutely clung onto them. The American Army arrived outside the well defended Breton ports of Brest and Lorient on 6 and 7 August respectively. The German forces in Brest would hold out until mid-September, while the garrisons in Lorient and St Nazaire did not surrender until the end of the war. This mattered little as by August Le Havre and Antwerp held much greater allure for the Allies.

Despite Churchill's efforts, Eisenhower won the day and Anvil became Dragoon, using the forces of General Alexander Patch's US 7th Army from Italy and General Jean de Lattre de Tassigny's French 2nd Corps, his units having been built up in North Africa following the invasion there. The landings were scheduled to take place on 15 August 1944, ten weeks after D-Day. There would be no stopping the fleet of two thousand Allied warships and landing craft bearing 151,000 American, British, Canadian and French troops.

American Sherman tanks gathered near Mondragone in Italy in the summer of 1944 for the invasion of the French Riviera known as Operation Dragoon.

LSTs (Landing Ship Tanks) loading lorries in Naples prior to the assault on southern France.

More LSTs loading in Italy for the invasion of southern France. Redeploying American and French units from the Italian campaign proved highly controversial and caused unending logistical difficulties.

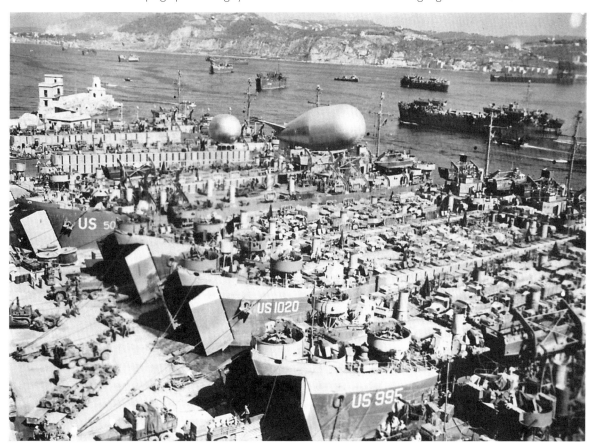

The Dragoon invasion fleet gathered off southern Italy. This force comprised 2,000 Allied ships and more than 150,000 troops.

General Johannes Blaskowitz, commander of Army Group G, defending southern France. Although Army Group G consisted of two armies, Blaskowitz lost all his armoured units to the fighting in Normandy following the D-Day landings. His infantry divisions were at best second-rate.

General Dwight D. Eisenhower, the Supreme Allied Commander, found himself at loggerheads with the British, who were opposed to the Riviera landings. For seven months in 1944 Ike endured unrelenting pressure from Monty and Churchill as they sought to strip away resources from Anvil/Dragoon, divert the invasion or cancel it altogether.

General Bernard Montgomery, seen here in conference with Eisenhower in Normandy, was largely indifferent to the invasion of southern France once Operation Overlord had taken place.

British Prime Minister Winston Churchill visiting General Omar Bradley, the commander of the US 1st Army in Normandy. Churchill did all he could to derail Operation Dragoon, arguing that the forces would better off left in Italy. On 7 August 1944 Winston spent the entire day lobbying Eisenhower to shift Dragoon to Brittany. Ike said no until he was 'practically limp'.

Free French light tanks of the 2nd Armoured Division rolling into Paris. The French army committed armoured divisions to both the Normandy and Riviera campaigns.

In Normandy and the Riviera Allied airborne forces were assisted by the FFI (French Forces of the Interior), directed by Gaullist General Koenig. As the summer of 1944 wore on they swelled the ranks of the Free French army, causing logistics headaches that greatly delayed the attack on the Franco-German border.

French half-tracks and an M8 Howitzer Motor Carriage belonging to the Free French 2nd Armoured Division parade in front of the Arc de Triomphe in Paris. While General de Gaulle's desire to liberate the French capital was understandable, the resulting delay greatly assisted German forces escaping eastwards towards the Low Countries and the German frontier.

Chapter Two

No Atlantic Wall

The French Riviera, once a byword for luxury, was host to German pillboxes, gun emplacements, mines and booby-traps, although Army Group G – or more precisely the 19th Army – was hardly in a fit state to defend it effectively. In addition, the German defences in southern France were incomplete and hardly comparable to the extensive Atlantic Wall that had been built along the northern French coast.

Generalfeldmarschall Gerd von Rundstedt, the German commander-in-chief (Oberbefehlshaber West), began to expect an Allied invasion of France after three panzer divisions rolled into neutral Vichy France on 11 November 1942 in response to the Allied landings in North Africa. The 69-year-old Rundstedt had commanded Army Groups during the conquest of Poland and France, and then led Army Group South during the successful overrunning of Ukraine, but had been dismissed by Hitler after being forced to retreat. Back in favour in July 1942, he had been appointed C-in-C West with responsibility for fortifying the whole of France against the anticipated Allied invasion. It was an impossible task.

Rundstedt's forces were divided into two Army Groups, the strongest of which was in the north. Generalfeldmarschall Erwin Rommel's Army Group B comprised General Friedrich Dollmann's 7th Army consisting of sixteen divisions stationed in northwestern France and General Hans von Salmuth's 15th Army consisting of twenty-five divisions stationed in Belgium and northeastern France. General Johannes Blaskowitz's Army Group G, with its headquarters in Toulouse, consisted of General Kurt von der Chevallerie's 1st Army and General Friedrich Wiese's 19th Army, totalling just seventeen divisions in all, stationed on the Biscay and Riviera coasts respectively. Wiese was based at Avignon northwest of Marseilles.

Blaskowitz's key armoured formations were the 11th Panzer and 17th SS Panzergrenadier Divisions under Chevallerie and the 2nd SS *Das Reich* and 9th Panzer Divisions under Weise. The latter, desperately in need of a refit and rest, had been sent to southern France under Generalleutnant Erwin Jolasse in March that year, where it absorbed the 155th Reserve Panzer Division. There were, in fact, only four infantry divisions of any note in the whole of southern France: the 708th, 242nd, 244th and 338th; the rest were refitting or forming.

The principal commands in the south were those of the 58th Reserve Panzer Corps, also stationed in Toulouse (controlling the 2nd SS Panzer Division, the 9th Panzer Division and the 189th Reserve Infantry Division), and General Ferdinand Neuling's 62nd Reserve Corps at Draguignan northeast of Toulon (controlling the 157th Reserve Infantry Division and the 242nd Infantry Division). Created in France in 1943, the 58th Corps was transferred from Rambouillet to Mödling in Austria before taking part in the occupation of Hungary in March 1944. The following month it returned to France, this time to Toulouse, coming under Blaskowitz's Army Group G.

Rundstedt expected that the Allies would attack the Pas de Calais as this was the shortest crossing point of the English Channel and just four days' march from the vital German industrial region of the Ruhr. The massing of the US 3rd Army and the Canadian 1st Army opposite the Pas de Calais convinced Rundstedt as well as Rommel (who took command of Army Group B, stretching from the Dutch border to the Loire in February 1944) and Hitler.

The net result was that Oberkommando der Wehrmacht (OKW – the Armed Forces High Command) gave priority to Salmuth's 15th Army north of the Seine. Due to the Allies' successful deception efforts, Rundstedt's better forces remained in the Pas de Calais area, which had a negative effect on Dollmann's 7th Army covering Normandy and Brittany. A phantom Allied 4th Army in Scotland also convinced the Germans of a threat to Norway, pinning down even more troops in Scandinavia. In the meantime Blaskowitz's Army Group was largely ignored.

A German Panzer Mk IV crew watch the scuttling of the French fleet at anchor in Toulon naval base. Following the Allied invasion of French North Africa in November 1942, Hitler occupied southern France, making him master of the whole country.

The French warship *Marseillaise* sinks in Toulon harbour.

The French fleet scuttled itself rather than fall into Hitler's hands. On the left is the warship *Strasbourg*; next to her, burning, is *Colbert*; under the smoke is *Algérie*; to the right is *Marseillaise*.

While Adolf Hitler viewed the defence of southern France as a low priority, he refused to let Army Group G withdraw to the north in the face of an anticipated Allied invasion of the Riviera. Once the Allies had secured French North Africa, they turned their attentions to Sicily and Italy, giving German troops in southern France a breathing space.

General Johannes Blaskowitz was a competent officer but with the resources at his disposal he knew that retreat was the only option in the face of Operation Dragoon.

Blaskowitz reviewing his troops. With his headquarters in Toulouse, his area of responsibility ran from Bordeaux in the west to Nice in the east. This was an impossibly large area to defend.

A captured German flak gun. In the run-up to Operation Dragoon, southern France was subjected to continuous heavy bombing raids.

In the prelude to the Riviera invasion, USAAF bombers, such as these Boeing B-17 Flying Fortresses, systematically struck the French and Italian Mediterranean coasts.

A B-17 nose gunner ready for action. The Luftwaffe was very weak in southern France and did little to impede the raids.

Despite conducting attacks along the entire French southern coast to confuse the Germans about possible locations for an invasion, the raids did indicate to Blaskowitz that an assault was imminent.

Chapter Three

Lost Panzers

The invasion in Normandy on 6 June 1944 quickly impacted on Blaskowitz's command as the French Resistance stepped up its efforts across France and many of his units were ordered north. The very day after D-Day the 17th SS Panzergrenadier Division received orders to depart its marshalling area and head for Normandy. Under the designation Operation Mimose (or Mimosa), the division redeployed from the area of General Chevallerie's 1st Army south of the Loire to the sector of General Dollmann's 7th Army facing Lieutenant-General Omar N. Bradley's US 1st Army at the base of the Cotentin peninsula.

General Heinz Lammerding, commanding the 2nd SS Panzer Division, was also ordered to Normandy, but his forces were already bogged down fighting the local Resistance units (Maquis). Large areas were under their control, leaving the German forces surrounded and cut off. Lammerding was soon signalling General Krüger in Toulouse with his catalogue of woes; he was understandably annoyed that his panzer division was wasting its valuable time fighting the Maquis, which was a role that should have been handled by local security divisions.

On top of this, only 40 per cent of Lammerding's panzers and 70 per cent of his half-tracks and prime movers were serviceable. Repeated calls for spare parts fell on deaf ears, which meant broken-down vehicles could not be moved and therefore required infantry to guard them. Six depots had to be set up for the waifs and strays, and efforts to commandeer local civilian vehicles produced few results. This was to be the typical experience of many of the units moving northwards to join the fighting in Normandy.

In response, General Blaskowitz requested OKW to provide troops to replace the 2nd SS once it had left Corrèze and Dordogne. A battle group from the 11th Panzer Division, comprising two infantry battalions, an artillery battalion and an anti-tank company, was assembled with instructions to contact the 2nd SS in Tulle. These forces arrived on 11 June and the 2nd SS duly rolled north to Limoges. The following day Blaskowitz himself took personal control of the anti-partisan operations and requested that OKW formally declare the southwest a battle zone. The French Resistance now found itself at war with Army Group G.

General Krüger's 58th Reserve Panzer Corps staff were then ordered to Le Mans to help direct the fight against the Americans. Krüger was an experienced tank commander, having been in command of the 1st Panzer Division from mid-July 1941 to the beginning of January 1944. His corps dropped its reserve designation on 6 July and departed on the 27th, joining Panzergruppe West two days later, although it was subsequently subordinated to the 7th Army and Panzergruppe Eberbach.

On 27 July 1944 the 9th Panzer Division was also put on notice to be ready to march north from the Avignon area. By 1 August it and six infantry divisions of varying quality were heading for the Normandy battlefield, now that it was clear to the Germans that the Americans' Operation Cobra represented a very real threat. As it rumbled northwards, the 9th Panzer Division was set upon by both the Maquis and Allied aircraft. Despite numerous air attacks, the division seemed to escape largely unscathed as it moved towards the Normandy battlefield, although in the event the division never got to fight as a whole, due to the belated destruction of the bridges over the Loire and the Allied landings in southern France. Elements of the support services never reached the division in Normandy and were not reunited with their parent formation until it had retreated to Metz following the defeat.

It was clear that Army Group G was haemorrhaging units it could ill afford to lose. As the deadline for Operation Dragoon loomed, Blaskowitz had very few panzers remaining in southern France. Most of his armoured divisions – the 2nd SS, 9th and 17th SS Panzergrenadier Divisions, along with elements of the 271st, 272nd, 276th and 708th Infantry Divisions – had already been drawn north to the fighting in Normandy. Only the 11th Panzer Division remained in the south, and it was refitting northeast of Bordeaux after being mauled on the Eastern Front. Blaskowitz had lost almost all his panzers, which meant he had very few tanks available to oppose landings in the Riviera or protect his withdrawal.

The best panzer in France in 1944 was the Panther but all available Panthers were deployed in northern France in an effort to contain the Normandy bridgehead. To try to stem the Allied advance, in the late summer of 1944 new panzer brigades were raised and equipped with Panther tanks but most were lost at Arracourt fighting Patton's US 3rd Army.

The 11th Panzer Division was mainly equipped with the Panzer Mk IV, the backbone of the panzer forces in France.

A GI with a captured German Hummel ('Bumble-Bee') self-propelled gun. Armed with a 150mm sFH18/1 L/70 field gun mounted on a Panzer IV chassis, the Hummel went into production in 1943. Typically, each panzer division received a battery of six Hummels. The 11th Panzer Division would lose most of its armoured fighting vehicles, especially running the American gauntlet at Montélimar.

The ubiquitous Stürmgeschutz III was deployed in the south of France. This one seems to have been cannibalised for spare parts as the front drive sprocket and fittings have been removed.

Lacking support from the Luftwaffe, Army Group G was reliant on flak panzers such as this Wirbelwind. It mounted a 20mm quad anti-aircraft gun on a Panzer IV hull and was converted from existing gun tanks from July to November 1944. These flak panzers were issued to the anti-aircraft platoons of the panzer divisions' tank regiments.

GIs give this German 37mm self-propelled flak gun the once-over.

Chapter Four

Dragoon's Shock and Awe

By the evening of 14 August 1944 no fewer than 526 C-47 transport aircraft and 452 Horsa and Waco gliders had been assembled to ferry the airborne assault force to the Riviera. Le May, sited just inland from the landing beaches, provided protection for the invasion area and access to the Argens valley corridor, and was therefore to be secured by Allied airborne troops.

The parachute assault on the Le Muy–Le Luc area was conducted by the 1st Airborne Task Force, comprising the British 2nd Independent Parachute Brigade, the US 517th Parachute Regimental Combat Team, and a composite US parachute/glider regimental combat team formed from the 509th Parachute Infantry Battalion, the glider-deployed 550th Airborne Infantry Battalion, and the 1st Battalion, 551st Parachute Infantry Regiment.

During the Allied naval build-up in the Mediterranean, the Luftwaffe kept General Weise appraised of developments, although neither he nor Blaskowitz knew where the blow would fall. They had insufficient forces to defend the entire coastline, but the heavy Allied bombing of Toulon and other targets in the days before the landings alerted Blaskowitz that something was likely to happen in this area. By 14 August, suspecting an imminent attack in the Marseilles–Toulon area, Blaskowitz moved the 11th Panzer and two infantry divisions east of the Rhône.

Churchill, always with one eye on history, accompanied the fleet on HMS *Kimberley*, but slept through the initial landings. Later, as he stood on deck watching the events unfold, passing American troops yelled 'Winnie! Winnie!', unaware that he had done everything in his power to stop Dragoon. Unimpressed, he retired to his cabin to read. He later noted bitterly, 'One of my reasons for making public my visit was to associate myself with this well-conducted but irrelevant and unrelated operation.'

Eisenhower's recollection of the situation was far more generous:

As usual the Prime Minister pursued the argument up to the very moment of execution. As usual, also, the second that he saw he could not gain his own way, he threw everything he had into support of the operation. He flew to the

Mediterranean to witness the attack and I heard that he was actually on a destroyer to observe the supporting bombardment when the attack went in.

The main assault commenced at 0800 on 15 August 1944. The US 3rd Infantry Division landed on the left at Alpha Beach (Cavalaire-sur-Mer), the 45th in the centre on Delta Beach (St Tropez) and the 36th on the right on Camel Beach (St Raphael). The 3rd struck the boundary between the German 242nd and 148th Infantry Divisions. French commando units landed between Cannes and Hyères, flanking the assault beaches.

While the Allied airborne landings suffered heavy losses (only 60 per cent of the paratroops landed on their drop zones and about fifty gliders were lost), the seaborne landings were largely unopposed. There was no firing on the Allied fleet and 40 per cent of the prisoners taken were anti-Soviet Russians who had volunteered to fight Stalin, but had found themselves in the south of France. Those who did offer token resistance were swiftly dealt with.

Captain Harry Butcher, Eisenhower's naval aide, recalled:

Today is D-Day for Anvil....We have just heard from Major General Alexander M. Patch, veteran of Guadalcanal, who commands the US 7th Army in the southern landings. He says the operation seems successful.

Our old friend Lucian Truscott is commanding the 6th Corps, which is comprised of the 3rd, 36th and 45th Divisions, which were the assault divisions. These were supported by airborne troops, Rangers, Commandos, French Commandos and the 1st Special Service under Major-General Robert T. Frederick (formerly of Operations Division). All assault divisions reported successful breaching of beach defences in target area and the attack was proceeding according to plan.

More than 94,000 men and 11,000 vehicles came ashore on that first day. The US 3rd and 45th Infantry Divisions were soon pressing towards Marseilles and the Rhône, while the 36th headed towards the Route Napoleon and Grenoble. The follow-up forces, including the US 6th Corps headquarters, the US 7th Army headquarters and the French 2nd Corps (1st Armoured, 1st and 3rd Algerian and 9th Colonial Divisions), came ashore the following day and passed through 6th Corps on the Marseilles road. Due to the rapidity of the advance, lack of fuel became a greater impediment than German resistance. What followed was dubbed 'the champagne campaign'.

General Weise tried to establish a defence line using the 242nd Infantry Division in the Toulon area, the 244th guarding Marseilles and elements of the 189th and

198th as they came across the Rhône. The failure of the German Mortain counterattack in Normandy and the developing Falaise Pocket meant that by 16 August it was imperative to save Blaskowitz's Army Group G before a more widespread collapse occurred in France.

C-47 Skytrains of the 81st Troop Carrier Squadron bearing US paratroops to their drop zones in the Le Muy–Le Luc area of southern France on 15 August 1944. These forces successfully surrounded General Neuling's 62nd Corps headquarters at Draguigan.

In contrast to Operation Overlord in Normandy and the subsequent Operation Market-Garden in the Netherlands, there was no worry about the airborne forces being confronted by panzers in the south of France.

After the medium and heavy bombers came the dive-bombers. Here, an F6F-5 Hellcat is about to fly from the escort carrier USS *Kasaan Bay* in support of Operation Dragoon. These aircraft attacked defences, airfields and any road traffic they could find.

The USS *Philadelphia*, a Brooklyn class light cruiser, opening fire with turrets four and five in the area of the Gulf of St Tropez. On 17 August 1944 *Philadelphia* provided support for French troops on the western outskirts of Toulon. Off the Normandy coast such firepower wreaked havoc amongst the panzers, but on the Riviera there were no Panzers anywhere near the beaches.

A transport ship preparing to unload its cargo. Keen to avoid another Anzio, the Allies knew that their armour must push inland as quickly as possible.

Infantry landing craft on the invasion beaches. The assault forces comprised US infantry divisions only; the armoured units followed later. There were not enough landing craft to conduct Operation Dragoon in parallel with D-Day, thereby nullifying any diversionary value it may have had.

Two Americans, killed while storming a German dugout, await collection.

An American casualty is evacuated. Allied casualties along the Riviera were light. Note the wire matting laid to make clearing the beach easier.

Trucks and lorries off-loading from an LST. Over 94,000 men and 11,000 vehicles came ashore on the first day.

More landing ships bringing men and equipment onto the Riviera's beaches.

The Allied build-up continued on 22 August 1944. The lower branches of the trees have been shorn of their foliage by the bombardment that preceded the invasion.

A DUKW amphibious truck bringing supplies ashore.

With the invasion beaches secure, more US infantry come ashore. This photo shows the US 3rd Infantry Division landing at Alpha Beach near Cavalaire.

Another DUKW photographed on 26 August, this time bringing blood and medical personnel onto the French beaches.

General Lucian Truscott, commander of the US 6th Corps, awarding a Bronze Star to one of his officers, Captain Richard Wolfer. Truscott had ample experience of amphibious operations, having taken part in the seaborne assaults on French Morocco, Sicily and the Italian mainland. He was understandably determined that Operation Dragoon should not turn into another Anzio, where the Allies had become hemmed in by counterattacking German armour. He wanted his tanks inland as swiftly as possible to destroy the German defence effort.

Chapter Five

Desperate Retreat

Following the Allies' successful landings in the south of France, the US 7th Army under General Patch was soon pushing up the Rhône valley towards Avignon, Montélimar and ultimately Lyon. Blaskowitz had to time his escape in such a way that his units did not either get ahead of themselves or fall too far behind, while drawing in his right flank and fending off the Americans and French on his left.

On 17 August Blaskowitz received his orders and abandoned Toulouse, withdrawing north. General Ferdinand Neuling's 62nd Corps at Draguignan, a few miles northwest of Le Muy, was not so lucky and his men found themselves surrounded by enemy paratroopers; his two infantry divisions became trapped at Marseilles and Toulon. Weise sent the 189th Infantry Division to clear Le Muy and relieve the 62nd Corps, but the Americans easily fended off the feeble counterattacks by elements of the 189th and 148th Divisions.

Blaskowitz was ordered to move his forces northeastwards, except for the 148th Division in the Cannes–Nice area and a reserve mountain division at Grenoble, both of which were instructed to move into Italy. Marseilles and Toulon were to be held as German fortresses. Overseeing the retreat up the west bank of the Rhône was General Petersen's 4th Luftwaffe Field Corps, while Kniess's 85th Corps was to manage things on the east bank. The plan was to coordinate their march on Lyon with the 64th Corps, which was heading the same way from the Atlantic Coast via central France with the remains of two infantry divisions. This combined force would then move north towards Dijon and make contact with the retreating Army Group B. Blaskowitz must have looked at his situation maps with an air of exasperation, since all this had to be achieved with General George Patton's US 3rd Army on the verge of seizing Lyon or Dijon and the US 7th Army pushing up behind from the Riviera.

In addition, both the 4th Luftwaffe Field Corps and the 85th Corps had to shepherd vulnerable retreating support personnel numbering about 100,000, including 2,000 women, all of whom had little or no combat value. These units had no more than rifles with which to protect themselves and were at risk from the vengeful French Resistance. Indeed, the presence of the Resistance ensured they could not flee northeastwards via the Massif Central, but had to detour via Poitiers and Bourges to Dijon.

Giving the withdrawal order to the 19th Army was easy as it shared Blaskowitz's Avignon headquarters, but the 64th Corps could not be raised on the radio. A liaison officer was sent by car to Toulouse, from where radio and courier messages could be sent out. Just to be on the safe side, a plane was also dispatched to Bordeaux. Despite all this, none of the messages got through, although by good fortune the naval station at Bordeaux received the order via Berlin.

Frustratingly, before its departure the 64th Corps was obliged to leave behind the better elements of two infantry divisions to hold the fortresses of Bordeaux-Gironde and La Rochelle. In the meantime the 159th Infantry Division formed the vanguard and the southern flank of this retreating corps, while the 16th Division acted as rearguard and screened the northern flank.

On 20 August the French 3rd Algerian Infantry Division reached Mont Faron on the outskirts of Toulon, where General de Lattre ordered de Monsabert's forces to Ange Pass in preparation for an assault on Marseilles to the west. By the 21st the German garrison at Toulon was completely surrounded and in the evening elements of the 3rd Algerian Light Infantry Regiment moved from the suburbs into the city itself and street fighting broke out. The last of the German units had surrendered by the 26th. The week-long battle for Toulon cost the French 2,700 casualties, but Blaskowitz's forces needlessly lost 17,000 men.

In Marseilles the Resistance did not stand idly by. The Communists took over the city's prefecture on 23 August as de Lattre's troops closed in on the suburbs. The garrison could have easily overwhelmed them but was more concerned with the approaching regular French army. Just two days after the fall of Toulon, and following an attack by the Algerians on the Notre Dame de la Garde feature, the Marseilles garrison also officially surrendered. Some 11,000 German troops laid down their weapons. The American and French armies found Marseilles already in the hands of a Resistance-led left-wing administration. Initially, cooperation between the American military and the French proceeded smoothly, but American plans for the port and their long-term presence soon strained relations, causing problems for the pursuit northwards.

Remarkably, French and American forces had captured both Toulon and Marseilles in just fourteen days. The planners, erring on the safe side, had assumed that they would not be secured until D plus 40. With all his formations ashore, de Lattre's Army B became the French 1st Army, consisting of the 1st Corps under General Béthouart on the right and the 2nd Corps under de Monsabert on the left. They would soon be snapping at Blaskowitz's heels.

Even as the Allies' bridgehead was being consolidated, in order to avoid the errors of the Anzio landings in Italy, it was decided that it was imperative for General Truscott's US 6th Corps to thrust northwards as quickly as possible. The Gap of Montélimar provided him with the best way of blocking Route N7 and trapping Wiese's escaping 19th Army.

The Rhône river flows in an almost straight north–south line for more than 200km between Lyon and its entrance to the delta at Avignon. Beyond Orange it narrows greatly, and some 70km north of Avignon at Montélimar the Montélimar Plain and the Valence Plain are divided by the Cruas Gorge, also known as the Gap (or Gate) of Montélimar. The west bank of the river is bordered by cliffs, while on the east deeply forested hills slope up to a height of some 400m.

To exploit his breach at the town of Gap, Truscott ordered his deputy corps commander Brigadier-General Frederick Butler and his task force (753rd Tank Battalion, 2nd Battalion, 143rd Infantry from the 36th Division, 59th Armoured Field Artillery Battalion, 117th Reconnaissance Squadron plus tank destroyers and supporting combat engineers) to spearhead the push.

The US 36th Infantry Division was to follow up towards Grenoble through Castellane and up the N85, while the 3rd and 45th Divisions pushed up the Argens corridor towards the Rhône. The 3rd Division rumbled along the N7, triumphantly forcing its way into Aix-en-Provence on 21 August. Everywhere the Germans seemed in disarray or had already moved on. The 45th Division secured the crossings over the Durance by clearing Barjols, which enabled the 3rd Division to shift right to join the march on Grenoble. Their job, if all went well, was to herd the fleeing Germans into the arms of Task Force Butler and the 36th Division at the Gap of Montélimar. A trap was being set to foil Blaskowitz's orderly withdrawal.

Futile German attempts to reinforce their troops facing the beachheads were soon thwarted once Task Force Butler had taken the Col de la Croix Haute mountain pass some 1,179m up on the N75 north of Apres. Similarly, with the aid of the Free French forces, Gap was taken along with 1,000 German prisoners. This meant that the German 157th Reserve Division at Grenoble could not send any further troops to the south.

Butler swung west to block the German escape routes up the Rhône valley. North of Livron, his units caught a German convoy of thirty vehicles with devastating results, but around La Coucourde they ran into superior German forces. By this stage the Germans had established themselves on the hills dominating the roads heading north and east, known as Ridge 300. However, on the 21st the Americans reached the high ground overlooking the Rhône valley north of the Gap of Montélimar. A desperate battle was now imminent.

American M3A3 or M5A1 light tanks pushing inland past a wrecked German Sd Kfz 11 semi-track. Within two days of the Allied invasion of the Riviera, Army Group G was in full retreat. Units had to be withdrawn from Bordeaux, Toulouse and Avignon.

German officers inspect Sd Kfz 251 armoured personnel carriers, used by panzergrenadiers, loaded onto railcars. The Ausf D seen here went into production in September 1943 and continued until the end of the war. Moving equipment by rail was not safe as it attracted air attack.

GIs inspect a German lorry caught in an air attack. As Army Group G withdrew northwards, American artillery and air strikes took their toll.

An American supply convoy pushing into the French interior. Capturing the southern French ports of Marseilles and Toulon was vital to ensure a swift Allied build-up on the Riviera. Supplying the Allied armies strung out across France would prove a major logistical challenge.

A German half-track towing a sFH18 150mm gun across an exposed bridge. This weapon formed the backbone of German medium artillery strength during the Second World War.

Frustratingly for General Blaskowitz, he was obliged to leave garrisons in La Rochelle, Bordeaux, Marseilles and Toulon. These inevitably had to surrender as the Allies advanced.

General de Lattre de Tassigny, Minister of War André Diethhelm and Emmanuel d'Astier de la Vigerie, Minister of the Interior, review French troops during the liberation ceremony in Marseilles on 29 August 1944.

Both Toulon and Marseilles were captured more quickly than had been anticipated.

Free French troops manhandle a captured Pak anti-tank gun in liberated Toulon; the battle for the 'fortress' city cost the French 2,700 casualties but yielded 17,000 German prisoners.

In total, 28,000 German troops surrendered to the French at Toulon and Marseilles.

A German StuG IV. Apart from the 11th Panzer Division, General Blaskowitz had few armoured units on the Riviera. Most of his assault gun battalions had been sent north to fight in Brittany and Normandy.

Charles de Gaulle with the Free French 2nd Armoured Division in Paris. Ultimately, the only people who benefited from the invasion of southern France were de Gaulle and Stalin. In particular, de Gaulle was able to take credit for liberating the key cities of Marseilles, Paris and Toulon.

A captured German StuG III Ausf G. Army Group G was desperately short of assault guns and panzers in southern France.

Chapter Six

The Battle for Montélimar

From the hills lining the Rhône valley north of Montélimar Task Force Butler's reconnaissance units watched enemy traffic stream up the main valley road, hampering the enemy armour trying to get there through Puy-St Martin. Along the floor of the valley itself the Germans had grouped around the 11th Panzer Division; in their path lay the American 636th Tank Destroyer Battalion and the 753rd and 191st Tank Battalions. The first real tank action of the campaign now commenced.

Butler's men opened up on the easy targets presented by the fleeing Germans below. A tank crewman attached to the 143rd Infantry Regiment recalled:

> We fired our guns continuously without stopping, and the recoil system got so hot that the system was slowing down. Norris, my loader, was pushing shells into the breach with his fist, and due to the fast fire, the skin began to peel off his hand. I exchanged places with Norris for a while, and I also lost some skin. We fired until we were out of ammunition and had to order more.

Just seven days after the landings the US 36th Infantry Division had penetrated 402km into France and reached Grenoble. Truscott instructed the 36th to obstruct the German withdrawal up the Rhône, as well as to counter any German reinforcements that might be pushing south, but the division was spread over four widely separated sectors: Grenoble itself, Gap and Guillestre, Digne, and in the beachhead.

In order to escape, Wiese's German 19th Army would have to barge the GIs of the 36th Infantry out of the way. By 1700 hours on 23 August a battalion from the 141st Infantry Regiment had got to within a kilometre of Montélimar before small-scale counterattacks developed along its flanks. By midnight, enemy infiltration threatened its supply lines and the battalion was forced to withdraw. The following day the entire division deployed to the region. The 142nd Infantry Regiment moved swiftly from Gap and Guillestre to defensive positions, while the 143rd hurried down from Grenoble.

Behind the 11th Panzer Division, reinforced and backed by fresh units, came the entire 198th Infantry Division, determined to break the American cordon. Just as the 198th mounted a full-scale attack to drive the 141st Infantry Regiment from its positions northeast of Montélimar and force its artillery to withdraw out of range of the highway, the 142nd and 143rd Regimental Combat Teams raced up from the south. On 24 August the 142nd reached the battleground and occupied defensive positions in an area some 40km long; it was followed by the balance of the 143rd.

From 25 to 30 August the 36th Division was attacked daily, with the main German effort pushing along a spur valley running northeastwards from Montélimar, in an attempt to cut the 36th's supply routes and encircle the defenders. In addition, the Germans constantly subjected the division's long defensive perimeter to spoiling attacks designed to prevent the 36th from launching any attacks of its own.

On the evening of 25 August Route Seven, several miles north of Montélimar, was severed by the entire 141st Regimental Combat Team, reinforced by elements of the 143rd. In the process they beat off German infantry and armour. Crucially this attack cut the valley road at a narrow neck of the Rhône south of La Coucourde.

Lieutenant-Colonel Charles Wilber's mission was to hold the block as long as possible. In the event of the Germans breaking through, he and his men were to fall back eastwards to Crest and hold the town at all costs, blowing up the bridges as a last resort. Subsequent German counterattacks did indeed break through the roadblock soon after midnight.

Alarmingly, German armour was soon being reported north and northwest of Crest, in the vicinity of Banlieu and near Grance. The northernmost roadblock, manned by the 36th Cavalry Reconnaissance Troop, was forced back at daybreak by overwhelming German power. Reinforcements in the shape of the 157th Infantry Regiment of the US 45th Division were quickly deployed north of Crest.

By now, although the 36th Division had almost surrounded the 19th Army, the Germans were on three sides of the division. Artillerymen turned their guns through 180 degrees to pummel the German armour threatening Grane and Crest to the north. The 36th Division's salient at Montélimar thrust towards Route Seven several miles north of the city. Running through Condillac, Sauzet and Cleon and anchored at Crest, the snaking lines of supply and communication ran from the south to Crest. At first the Germans held the initiative and if they had conducted a bold oblique thrust to the east, they might have disrupted the whole of 6th Corps, cutting the only artery up from the beaches.

General Dahlquist decided to hold the little Rubion streambed (in front of a vital supply road) on a flat bowl-shaped plain backed up by a wall of hills. His divisional artillery was deployed onto the hills opening up in a great arc to the south, west and north. Key terrain held by the infantry allowed gun positions to be disposed in such a manner that the route of German withdrawal along the Rhône was under fire for 25km, creating a perfect killing field.

The fleeing German convoys were now blasted off the roads, and the entire zone was literally covered with a mass of burned-out vehicles, abandoned equipment, dead men and animal carcasses. German attacks, initiated simultaneously from three directions, were hammered and repulsed by the same paralysing artillery barrages. On the Rhône side of the line the 36th Division committed to putting a final seal on the main valley highway. In addition, American P-47 fighters swooped in, pounded and destroyed all the bridges across the river, forcing the enemy to remain on the east bank.

Trapped in the developing pocket were three German divisions hell-bent on holding open their escape route. On two successive days regiments of the German 198th Division charged against the centre of the Rubion line at Bonlieu and were thrown back by battalions of the 143rd and 142nd. The 141st, in the hot seat near the Rhône, faced incessant enemy attacks striving to brush them away from Route Seven.

Further American efforts to seize La Coucourde and to recapture and block Route Seven were not completely successful, although much damage was inflicted on the enemy. The 3rd Battalion of the 143rd held the vital Magranon Ridge near La Coucourde, overlooking Route Seven, during three days of critical fighting. Despite being cut off and isolated in small groups, the battalion fought on to defeat decisively the exhausted German forces. Towards the end of the fighting divisional forces were shifted northwards to strike again along the Drome river valley.

For nine days the Germans fought the GIs before retreating on Lyon. In particular, on 25 August the 11th Panzer Division and supporting units launched five attacks. Two days later the bulk of the 11th Panzer Division and most of the retreating infantry had crossed the Rhône north of Drome, having lost 2,500 men taken prisoner, leaving the Montélimar region in the hands of General Baptist Kniess's fresh 85th Corps.

General Otto Richter's 198th Infantry Division remained at Montélimar, with a rearguard engineer detachment to the south. On the night of 27/28 August Richter led his remaining two regiments and other survivors in a bid to escape but they ran straight into the US 36th Division's push on the town. Richter himself and some 700 of his men were captured, but not before the Americans suffered around 100 casualties in a fierce firefight.

The 143rd Regiment shattered German forces around Loriol on 29 August, taking more than 1,000 prisoners in the final mop-up. Also that day the 142nd seized Livron, but straggling groups of Germans continued to resist strongly until the 30th. Then elements of the 3rd Division, pressing the Germans from the south, contacted the 141st near Clary.

Despite the terrible destruction wrought on the 19th Army, on the last day of the battle Colonel Paul Adams, commanding the 143rd, reported to headquarters: 'I'm expecting a hell of a fight.' At 0600 hours the last German counterattack formed up in the vicinity of La Coucourde, but within an hour it had been repulsed, the attackers destroyed or captured.

It was American artillery at Montélimar that counted most and swayed the tide of battle. During eight days of fighting the 36th Infantry's 131st, 132nd, 133rd and 155th field artillery battalions fired well over 37,000 rounds at the confined, retreating German troops. Supporting fire from the attached 41st, 977th and 93rd Armored Battalions brought the total number of rounds expended to considerably more than 75,000. It is a wonder that any German soldiers survived to fight another day.

The US 6th Corps' newspaper, *The Beachhead News*, reported triumphantly:

> Under the 36th Division command . . . such a great force of artillery was directed on the Germans that more than four thousand vehicles, one 380mm and five other railroad guns were destroyed, and the main escape gap for the fleeing German army was under constant fire and attack . . . the Division moved in and finished off the kill.

By the time the Battle for Montélimar ended, the 6th Corps had suffered 1,575 casualties, having inflicted five times that number on the Germans. For 18km north and south of the town the highway was a smoking double-column of knocked-out vehicles, dead horses and men. There was no stretch of road that did not contain some degree of destruction.

In total, Blaskowitz and Wiese's troops suffered 11,000 casualties and lost 1,500 horses. The Americans took some 5,000 prisoners at Montélimar and destroyed more than 4,000 vehicles, as well as the 189th and 338th Divisions. The Allies secured the region between Nice and Avignon as far north as Briançon via Grenoble to Montélimar, mauling General Wiese's 19th Army mainly through artillery and air strikes as it sought to flee. As a result the Germans were unable to draw up an effective defensive line until after the Americans had crossed the Moselle river.

Although dubbed the 'Champagne Campaign', the liberation of southern France was still a bloody affair. The Americans and French sustained about 10,000 casualties.

American Shermans with the tank battalion supporting the US infantry divisions soon found themselves tangling with the 11th Panzer Division at Montélimar.

French civilians watch a passing American anti-tank gun and crew.

The battle for Montélimar would cost the US 6th Corps almost 1,600 casualties. Fighting in urban areas always incurred high losses.

The FFI punishes a French woman for consorting with the enemy in newly liberated Montélimar.

An American heavy machine gun team keeping watch. Three American Regimental Combat Teams blocked the Germans' escape route at Montélimar.

The remains of a Panzer Mk IV. The 11th Panzer and 198th Infantry Divisions fought hard to keep open Route Seven to the north of Montélimar to safeguard the 19th Army's retreat.

A devastated column of German horse-drawn wagons and lorries outside Montélimar. Blaskowitz's forces held the town until 28 August 1944, when General Otto Richter was captured. The Americans took 5,000 prisoners and destroyed more than 4,000 vehicles.

This StuG III has clearly been requisitioned by the US Army. This type of assault gun was ideal for the defensive battles fought in France.

American tankers examining an abandoned StuG III assault gun.

French troops with a captured Panzer IV/70(A) tank destroyer. Fewer than 300 examples of this particular variant were ever built. In contrast, more than 900 IV/70(V) were produced. During the fighting in Lorraine both the 3rd and 15th Panzergrenadier Divisions each had a battalion of these powerful tank destroyers.

Chapter Seven

Blaskowitz's Falaise

The retreating Germans conducted a number of delaying actions, notably in the Autun and Dijon regions, but ultimately they were now being driven from the whole of France. On 30 August the 4th Luftwaffe Field Corps reached Lyon, where it found the city's anti-aircraft defences had been fending off French troops to the west. The corps was transferred to the east bank of the Rhône, where it joined units of the 11th Panzer Division. However, elements of the 4th Corps straggling behind were marshalled on the west bank to cover the 85th Corps.

In Lyon itself the US 36th Infantry Division found the Maquis and the Milice – the Vichy police, whom the French hated as much as they did the Germans, battling it out. The factories on the city's outskirts were burning and all the bridges had been destroyed except one. While the fighting in the industrial area was on-going, across the river patrols were greeted by great crowds of cheering civilians. The jeeps were surrounded by masses of men and women who just wanted to shake an American hand or stare curiously at their liberators.

The US 7th Army liberated Lyon on 3 September and another 2,000 Germans were captured; just four days later Besançon was also liberated. There were two days of celebrations in Lyon and all sorts of parties in honour of the Americans, including drinking bouts in which the French and their guests vied with one another in paying extravagant compliments. Every private home threw open its doors to the liberators.

Meanwhile on the eastern flank the German 148th Reserve Division delayed the Americans once they were over the Var river. Their task was greatly assisted by the Maritime Alps, which run northwards to the Cottian and Graian Alps south of Geneva. The Germans had established defensive positions along the Menton–Sospel–Breil road, the Nice–Ventimiglia highway and the Turini Pass. The division was eventually incorporated into the new 75th Corps tasked with defending northwest Italy and preventing the Allies turning the Italian Front. By 8 September the Americans had pushed west of Nice and reached Menton and the Italian border. The advance then came to a halt as there was some concern that the US 5th and British 8th Armies might drive the Germans out of Italy via the Franco-Italian border.

On the 12th the victorious Allied forces in southern and northern France linked up at Châtillon-sur-Seine as de Lattre's forces made contact with General Leclerc's French 2nd Armoured Division, part of Patton's US 3rd Army. Luckily for Blaskowitz, the latter had been starved of gasoline in favour of General Montgomery's forces. Patton came to a stop at Verdun and for five days his forces were left kicking their heels just 112km from the Rhine.

Some 31,000 German prisoners were taken at St Tropez, Toulon and Marseilles, with a further 2,500 around Montélimar; another 12,000 Germans surrendered during the Allied drive north from Lyon and another 20,000 were cut off west of Dijon. Army Group G lost another 10,000 men to Patton's US 3rd Army and another 25,000 were left in Atlantic garrisons. It has been estimated that the Germans lost up to 7,000 dead in southern France and about 21,000 wounded. In total, then, Blaskowitz lost perhaps half of his 250,000 troops. The Americans suffered about 4,500 casualties and the French a slightly higher number. Nevertheless, both Army Group G and the 19th Army escaped as coherent formations. Unfortunately the French 2nd Armoured Division's actions in liberating Paris helped prolong the war, for the delay round the city enabled a greater part of Army Group G's 1st Army to escape intact over the Rhine. After the collapse in Normandy, Field Marshal Walter Model's Army Group B, with four armies, was trying to stabilise the situation, defending the region from the North Sea down to Nancy.

The remains of Wiese's command streamed north to join Chevallerie's 1st Army, which was evacuating southwestern France and heading for the strategic Belfort Gap – the gateway to Germany just north of the Swiss border. The 11th Panzer Division, conducting a fighting retreat, withdrew to Alsace to defend the Belfort Gap in September. The Gap forms the pass between the French Jura and Vosges mountains and the Germans knew that if they lost control of it, Strasbourg and all Würtemberg to the east would be exposed. The mountains consist of the High and Low Vosges, divided by the Saverne Gap. The Belfort Gap lies at the southern end of the High Vosges, the main route of approach to the Plain of Alsace. The lynchpin of the High Vosges is Epinal on the Moselle, which has two major routes through the mountains, one to Strasbourg and the Rhine and the other to Colmar and the Alsace Plain.

By early September Blaskowitz's 1st Army, now under General Otto von Knobelsdorff, was safely behind the Moselle and Wiese's 19th Army was holding Army Group G's front from Nancy to the Swiss border. Following Blaskowitz's successful withdrawal from southern France, Hitler was convinced he would be the man to oversee a much-needed counterblow in Lorraine.

Indeed, Hitler was hoping to decisively counter Patton, who was spearheading the Allies' eastward drive into Lorraine, which was posing a direct threat to the Westwall. However, until General Jacob L. Devers' US 6th Army Group, pushing up from the south of France, could nip off the remaining bulge formed by the German 19th Army, Patton's left flank was precariously exposed.

Despite the failure of the Normandy Mortain armoured counterattack, Hitler remained convinced that his panzers could successfully envelop the advancing Allies. This view was based on the German army's performance on the Eastern Front, where time and time again it had managed to snatch victory from the jaws of defeat, and not on the reality of the situation in France, where Operations Overlord and Dragoon were backed by overwhelming firepower on the ground and in the air.

Colonel Hans von Luck from the 21st Panzer Division, a veteran of the brutal fighting in Normandy and around the ancient city of Caen, bumped into General Hasso von Manteuffel in the Vosges on 9 September. In their discussions Manteuffel did not mince his words:

> The US 6th Army Group, including the French 1st Army, is approaching from southern France and is supposed to join up with Patton. The remains of our retreating armies from the Mediterranean and Atlantic coast are … still holding a wedge that extends as far as Dijon, but for how much longer?
>
> The worst of it is, Hitler is juggling with divisions that are divisions no more. And now Hitler wants to launch a panzer attack from the Dijon area to the north, in order, as he likes to put it, 'to seize Patton in the flank, cut his lines of communication, and destroy him'. What a misjudgement of the possibilities open to us.

With the docks damaged at Marseilles and Toulon, the Allies had to continue off-loading equipment on the Riviera beaches. These photos show amphibious US DUKWs running a continuous shuttle service.

The open French countryside left Army Group G vulnerable to air attack as it withdrew towards the German border.

The remains of a German vehicle still smouldering after an air strike.

The American and French tankers did not have it all their own way, as this burnt-out M4 Sherman testifies.

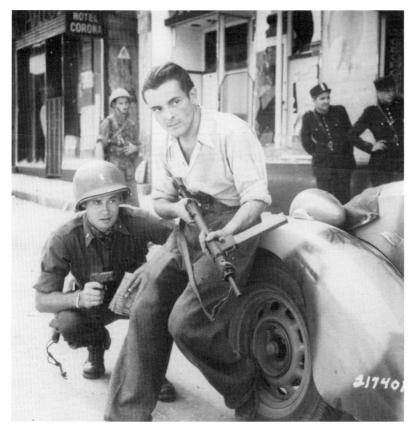

The FFI or French Resistance did all it could to harass the German withdrawal and assisted with the liberation of many cities and towns.

A German fatality rests not far from his vehicle. While the fighting in southern France was not on the same scale as in Normandy, it was just as brutal.

Withdrawing German units knew it was wise to bypass French villages where they were likely to be ambushed.

The speed of the liberation of southern France surprised everyone.

Army Group G's greatest losses were as a result of its personnel being captured – many of them were cut off and had little prospect of rescue. More than 75,000 Germans surrendered, 28,000 were killed or wounded, and 25,000 were left to garrison the Atlantic ports.

Few towns and villages escaped the fighting unscathed.

Chapter Eight

Disaster at Arracourt

Hitler hoped a decisive blow against Patton's advancing tanks would stop him getting into Germany and would prevent Devers' army group from linking up with Bradley's 12th Army Group. To this end he gave priority to his forces in Lorraine. In contrast, the Allies were now at the end of their supply lines and Allied supreme commander Dwight Eisenhower's attention was focusing on Operation Market Garden, which was intended to take Montgomery's 21st Army Group through the Netherlands and over the Rhine. Operations in the south were now just an unwanted distraction, although Patton was constantly calling for more fuel and ammunition in order to press on.

Hitler's forces in Lorraine were on the whole under-strength and of poor quality. Only the 16th Infantry Division with about 7,000 men was worthy of any note; the other units had been mauled in the fighting during the summer or were newly raised Volksgrenadier divisions of questionable value. Frightened recruits and weary veterans were hardly an ideal combination. In contrast, Patton's divisions were largely up to strength and eager to fight.

It was apparent that Hitler needed to act quickly or lose the initiative. Gathering a number of newly raised panzer brigades, he planned to surround Patton using the battered 5th Panzer Army, which had only recently escaped from the chaos of Normandy. In addition, General Blaskowitz was ordered to commit his only armoured unit, the veteran 11th Panzer Division, which was defending the Belfort Gap.

Hitler, as always obsessed with counterattacking when such action was simply not feasible, felt that the bridgehead west of Dijon would provide not only a haven for the 64th Corps but also a jumping-off point for an attack on Patton's southern front. Blaskowitz, looking at his situation reports, doubted the counterattack could succeed, while the ability to hold the area until the 64th Corps arrived was of even greater concern. He knew, however, that Hitler's orders could not be ignored and on 4 September he instructed the 47th Panzer Corps into the Neufchateau region. This, though, proved impossible in the face of attacks by the US 12th and 20th Corps.

Now under Manteuffel, the 5th Panzer Army was redeployed from Belgium to

Alsace-Lorraine. The counterattack was initially to involve three panzergrenadier divisions – the 3rd, the 15th (brought up from Italy) and the 17th SS (from Normandy) – plus the newly raised Panzer Brigades 111, 112 and 113. They were to be supported by elements of the Panzer Lehr, 11th and 21st Panzer Divisions and the new Panzer Brigades 106, 107 and 108. On paper at least, this seemed a credible force.

In total, however, Blaskowitz and Manteuffel were able to muster at most about 350 tanks. This amounted to barely three weak panzer divisions or a panzer corps – hardly sufficient for Hitler's optimistic plans. Against them Patton could field 1,122 M4 Sherman medium tanks and M10 and M18 tank destroyers. In addition, the 19th Army had just 165 artillery pieces; the rest lay scattered about southern France. The two German generals could see only one outcome.

Manteuffel's army was far from reconstructed following its defeat in Normandy. The panzer forces were in a poor state. The 17th SS Panzergrenadier Division, for example, had been boosted with reinforcements from units as far away as the Balkans and Denmark. It was able to field just four Panzer Mk IVs and twelve StuG III assault guns. The 21st Panzer Division had also been mauled in Normandy and could only muster a few assault guns.

The 11th Panzer Division was regarded as the best armoured unit in the region, but it too had lost a number of its tanks during its withdrawal from the south. For the Lorraine offensive it would be able to field about fifty panzers, over half of which were Panthers, but it would have to redeploy before it could have any bearing on the fighting. In contrast, the 3rd and 15th Panzergrenadier Divisions were in good order and up to strength. The former had a battalion of assault guns and the latter could field thirty-six Panzer Mk IVs; both also had a battalion of powerful Panzer IV/70 tank destroyers.

While the Nazi weapons factories alleviated the critical shortage of panzers on the Western Front following Falaise, there was little Hitler could do about his complete lack of experienced tank crews. In addition, his senior generals could see little point in raising new panzer brigades when the replacement panzers would have been better issued to the existing depleted panzer divisions.

Instead, the bulk of these new panzer brigades was raised from units that had been destroyed when the Red Army crushed Army Group Centre with Operation Bagration in June 1944. For example, Panzer Brigade 106 was created around the battered remnants of Panzergrenadier Division Feldherrnhalle. Also the first batch of brigades consisted only of single tank battalions. Again it was felt by some that the Eastern Front veterans would be better assimilated into existing units rather than formed into new stand-alone brigades.

With the Allies preoccupied in the south of France, Hitler knew he need not worry about the Italian front. In fact, Field Marshal Kesselring was directed to relinquish his 3rd and 15th Panzergrenadier Divisions to France and the Hermann Goering Panzer Division to Poland. These two panzergrenadier units would form the core of Hitler's opposition to Patton's US 3rd Army's push on the Upper Meuse.

Just as the Americans were losing momentum, Hitler planned to stop the US 3rd and 7th Armies from linking up by cutting off those forces pushing towards the Belfort Gap. This was to be done by a counterattack from Pontalier towards Plateau de Langres scheduled for 12 September. In the event, with the Americans converging on Dijon, these plans were quickly derailed. American military activity in the Nancy area likewise soon thwarted Hitler's plans for an armoured counterattack in Lorraine as Blaskowitz struggled to contain the US forces spilling over the Moselle. Although Hitler's counterattack was intended to cut off the US 3rd Army, Blaskowitz was more anxious that it should prevent an American wedge driving in between his 1st and 19th Armies.

Nancy was the lynchpin and in the subsequent fighting for the city Blaskowitz was forced to commit his available armoured forces. Between Metz to the north and Nancy lay the 3rd and 17th SS Panzergrenadier Divisions, while the 553rd Volksgrenadiers defended Nancy itself. Just to the south were deployed the 15th Panzergrenadiers, then Panzer Brigade 112, the 21st Panzer and Panzer Brigade 111. Panzer Brigade 113 was near Belfort, along with the 11th Panzer Division.

Under mounting pressure, it was not long before Blaskowitz and Manteuffel fell out. The 5th Panzer Army had to share control of the front with Blaskowitz's 1st and 19th Armies, causing administrative headaches for Knobelsdorff and Wiese. When Manteuffel visited Blaskowitz on 11 September both knew Hitler's plans were absolute nonsense. General Walter Botsch, the 19th Army's chief of staff, described their remaining troops as 'badly battered weak units and security forces, very poorly equipped with artillery and anti-tank material and in no position to resist the enemy'. Blaskowitz had no choice but to seek authorisation to withdraw towards the Vosges mountains.

In addition, the US 1st Army was bearing down on the German city of Aachen, causing Field Marshal von Rundstedt to redirect all available forces there, including Panzer Brigades 107 and 108. This meant that a third of the panzer brigade counteroffensive force was lost already. Rundstedt, after being sacked over Normandy, had found himself reappointed as CinC West in early September with orders to try to stop the rot.

In the meantime Panzer Brigade 106 was smashed while attempting to prevent the Americans from reaching the Moselle on 8 September. Two days later the US 4th Armored Division and the 35th 'Sante Fe' Infantry Division crossed the river south of Nancy in the face of fierce resistance from the 15th Panzergrenadiers. The next day the US 80th 'Blue Ridge' Infantry Division crossed to the north of the city and on 13 September faced a counterattack by the 3rd Panzergrenadiers with ten assault guns. That day, now that his defences had been ruptured, Blaskowitz gave the order to start evacuating Nancy, with the 553rd Volksgrenadier Division covering the withdrawal.

Elements of General Leclerc's French 2nd Armoured Division then crushed Panzer Brigade 112 at Dompaire, southwest of Nancy and northwest of Belfort, on 13 September. His Combat Command Langlade, slipping between Kampfgruppe Ottenbacher and the German 16th Infantry Division, took control of the high ground overlooking Dompaire. Following an American air strike, Panzer Brigade 112's Panthers were hemmed in on three sides. German reinforcements in the shape of forty-five Panzer Mk IVs from Panzer Regiment 2112 almost threatened to trap one of the French battle groups. Luckily, a French roadblock formed by armour and anti-tank guns beat off the German reinforcements and by the end of the day the panzer brigade had lost thirty-four Panthers and the panzer regiment twenty-eight Panzer Mk IVs. In total, Panzer Brigade 112 was reduced from ninety tanks to just twenty-one and suffered some 1,350 killed or wounded; the survivors were merged into the 21st Panzer. At least three Panthers involved in the Lorraine tank battles survived, including a Panther Ausf G which the French 2nd Armoured Division captured at Dompaire; it is now preserved at the French tank museum at Saumur. Blaskowitz and Manteuffel had lost four panzer brigades before their counteroffensive had even started. The 5th Panzer Army was left with just two panzer brigades – and the writing was clearly on the wall for Hitler's Lorraine operations.

Blaskowitz was well aware that he could not completely defy Hitler's plan to strike at the southern flank of Patton's 3rd Army, but the reality was that he no longer controlled the advanced bridgehead assembly area and had insufficient armoured units to mount such an operation. On 14 September he let Field Marshal Rundstedt know that the proposed offensive by the 5th Panzer Army was simply impossible, but that he could counterattack east of the Moselle river. Blaskowitz was of the opinion that Metz would provide a good rallying point, and as a strongpoint would hold Patton up until mid-December.

With the remaining German garrison at Nancy under threat of encirclement by the US 4th Armored Division, Blaskowitz threw the 3rd and 15th Panzergrenadiers into the counterattack. They suffered heavy casualties and the US 80th 'Blue Ridge' Division rolled into the city on 15 September. Task Force Sebree from the US 35th Infantry Division also entered the city, only to find that the Germans had already abandoned it.

When Manteuffel's delayed counteroffensive finally got under way on 18 September, Panzer Brigade 113 ran straight into the Americans at Lunéville southeast of the city and was forced to disengage. The brigade was then redirected to attack towards Arracourt east of Nancy, along with Panzer Brigade 111, although the latter became lost.

That night Blaskowitz ordered Manteuffel to continue the attack in the morning, 'without regard to the losses already suffered or the crippled condition of the 113 Panzer Brigade'. Manteuffel, aware that Blaskowitz was sticking slavishly to the dictates of Hitler and his high command, but concerned for his troops, branded the attack 'an outright waste of men and material'. In his chance meeting with Manteuffel, veteran Hans von Luck had damned Hitler's plan to attack Patton's flank as 'senseless and unrealistic' and 'illusory'.

During 19 September American tanks and artillery knocked out forty-three tanks, but Blaskowitz instructed Manteuffel to persist with the futile attack the following day. General von Mellenthin recalled: 'Our Panthers were superior to the American Shermans, but the enemy had very strong artillery and anti-tank support, and when the fog lifted enjoyed all the benefits of overwhelming air power. The German attack cost nearly fifty tanks and achieved nothing.'

Despite Blaskowitz's orders, Panzer Brigade 113 did little and 111 committed only a few companies to the fighting. There was now a danger that Patton would indeed drive a wedge between the 5th Panzer Army and the 1st Army and force its way to the Rhine.

Blaskowitz held Manteuffel responsible for this mess, while the latter blamed the poor results on the inexperienced panzer brigade crews. Hitler was so angry that his new panzer force had been squandered to no effect that he sacked the unfortunate commander of Army Group G. Blaskowitz's other 'crime' was quarrelling with Hitler's right-hand man Heinrich Himmler about the construction of second-line defences.

Despite successfully extricating Army Group G from the French Riviera, Hitler held Blaskowitz personally responsible for the failure of his panzer offensive in the Lorraine. At Hitler's headquarters General von Mellenthin recalled:

> In a voice ringing with indignation, Hitler severely criticised the way Blaskowitz had commanded his forces, and reproached him with timidity and lack of offensive spirit. In fact he seems to have thought that Blaskowitz could have taken Patton's Third Army in the flank and flung it back to Reims.

Hitler was deluded if he thought Blaskowitz had the resources to achieve such a feat. The German Army Personnel Office recorded dryly: 'When it became apparent that the retreat actions and measures taken by Army Group G were not in accordance with the way Hitler expected it to be, Hitler ordered Colonel General Blaskowitz . . . relieved.'

Mellenthin was appalled by the ungrateful treatment handed out to Blaskowitz and saw darker forces at work:

> He had just extricated his army group from the south of France under extremely difficult conditions, but his offence was that he had quarrelled with Himmler, first in Poland and recently in Alsace. Like so many others, Blaskowitz was made a scapegoat for the gross blunders of Hitler and his entourage.

Blaskowitz was sent home to Dresden, and his wife later wrote to relatives saying, 'Hans is now at home, planting cabbages.'

By 25 September the 11th Panzer Division had arrived, but with the new panzer brigades already cut to pieces, Manteuffel could muster only fifty tanks. For the attack north of Arracourt that day the 11th Panzer only had sixteen panzers and two regiments of panzergrenadiers, but they fought on for another four days against the US 4th Armored Division. The 559th Volksgrenadiers were also obliged to renew their attack against the US 35th Infantry Division.

The remains of Panzer Brigades 111, 112 and 113 were assigned to the 11th Panzer Division, the 21st Panzer Division and the 15th Panzergrenadiers respectively. The US 3rd Army had now gone over to the defensive and American withdrawals enabled Manteuffel to occupy Juvelize and Coincourt east of Arracourt. German attacks on 27 September to take Hills 318 and 293 ultimately ended in failure, despite the best efforts of the 11th Panzer Division, with the loss of twenty-three panzers.

By the end of the month the confused fighting in Lorraine between General Balck's Army Group G and Patton's US 3rd Army had dwindled into a general stalemate. Nonetheless, from an overall force of 616 panzers and assault guns committed in Lorraine, only 127 remained operational, although another 148 were repairable. Balck visited Rundstedt at Bad Kreuznach on the 29th and informed him that Army Group G needed a minimum of 140 panzers as well as artillery otherwise all its offensive operations would rapidly come to a standstill.

Rundstedt made it clear that Hitler was currently preoccupied with Aachen and Arnhem, and that there would be no reinforcements. In response, Balck instructed Manteuffel to break off his attacks and withdraw the exhausted 11th Panzer Division in order to husband his dwindling resources. Thus ended Hitler's ill-fated and ill-conceived attempts to cut off Patton's armoured spearhead.

Patton, with a three to one advantage in men, eight to one advantage in tanks and a huge superiority in artillery, struck on 8 November between Nancy and Metz with all the force he could muster. Although the Germans were taken by surprise, the bad weather hampered Patton's advancing armour. The 11th Panzer Division counterattacked two days later, claiming thirty American tanks destroyed. Having rescued the shaken 559th Volksgrenadier Division, the panzers then withdrew on Morhange.

The Germans counterattacked again on 12 November, capturing an entire American battalion. Although the Germans abandoned Morhange, Patton was forced to call a halt to his offensive. On the night of 17/18 November the 1st Army withdrew, leaving the ill-equipped 10,000-strong Metz garrison to its fate. In the event, the last of the city's forts did not surrender until 13 December. In the meantime Leclerc's French armour rolled into Strasbourg on 24 November.

Following the Riviera landings, Eisenhower wanted the US 6th and 12th Army Groups to link up in Lorraine but Hitler sought to prevent this.

After Patton's breakout from the Normandy bridgehead, his tanks sped eastwards through Lorraine. This threatened Hitler's defences on the Franco-German border. However, Patton was continually competing for resources, particularly fuel, with the other Allied armies, which hampered his progress.

An American Sherman crew try to retrieve their stranded tank. Judging from the stacked shells, this tank was being used in a fire support role.

German Höcker, or concrete Dragon's teeth, forming an anti-tank barrier along the Siegfried Line or Westwall protecting the German frontier. Note how the obstacles are taller at the back. Hitler's intention was to keep Patton away from the border by attacking him in Lorraine.

This Panther Ausf G, abandoned west of Metz, belonged to Panzer Brigade 106. The deployment of these half a dozen newly raised panzer brigades proved disastrous, as the crews were poorly trained and lacked adequate support. Many of them simply blundered into battle, often exposing the Panther's thin side armour to deadly enemy fire.

Although in the right hands the Panther was ferocious, the lack of experienced *panzertruppen* meant they suffered heavy losses at Arracourt fighting the poorly armoured and poorly armed Shermans.

US armour crossing the Siegfried Line in September 1944. This success was short-lived thanks to the subsequent heavy fighting in the Hürtgen Forest and the Ardennes.

Japanese–American troops of the 442nd Regimental Combat Team became embroiled in the Vosges campaign. The mountains were far from ideal for armoured warfare, leaving the infantry to bear the brunt of the fighting.

An American half-track negotiates a river of mud. While Patton's US 3rd Army was fighting in Lorraine, Bradley's US 1st Army became embroiled in the battle for the Hürtgen Forest – on German soil – in September 1944 that dragged on into the New Year.

Conditions for the US and French forces in the mountains were particularly harsh during the winter of 1944/5.

German artillery resisting the American advance in the Hürtgen Forest in November 1944.

An M10 Wolverine tank destroyer from the Régiment Blindé de Fusiliers Marins, Free French 2nd Armoured Division, photographed outside Halloville, France, on 13 November 1944.

American GIs rummage through the contents of a captured Panzer Mk IV. During the engagements at Arracourt against the US 4th Armored Division, the 11th Panzer Division was desperately short of tanks. The newly raised independent panzer brigades lost their Panthers thanks to inexperienced crews coming up against tough American and French tankers.

Chapter Nine

The Belfort Gap

With Hitler's withdrawing armies being pressed from the west and the south, their only remaining escape route from southern France lay in the network of roads and rail lines located in the 24km-wide Belfort Gap, between the Vosges mountains to the north and the Jura mountains to the southeast. Since the days of the Roman Empire this had formed a strategic corridor connecting the Paris basin and the Rhine valley.

This area also holds the principal tributary of the Rhône, namely the headwaters of the Saone-Doubs river. The latter's river valley formed the natural route that General Patch's US 7th Army would have to follow north. The region was ideal for FFI guerrilla activity as the hilly and heavily forested countryside is crisscrossed with numerous streams and rivers, and provided ideal locations for ambushes and other acts of sabotage.

While the Americans and French regrouped, Blaskowitz was granted a much-needed breathing space, which gave him time to create an effective defensive line. General Wiese recalled: 'It was an enigma to the Army, why the enemy did not execute the decisive assault on Belfort between 8 and 15 September 1944 through a large-scale attack.' The delay meant that the tired American and French troops lost their window of opportunity.

After landing on the French Riviera on 15 August 1944, the advance of the seven divisions of General Jean de Lattre de Tassigny's French 1st Army and the fourteen divisions of Patch's US 7th Army was very swift. Bypassing Toulon and Marseilles, the lead elements of the 7th Army had reached Grenoble by the 22nd with the objective of linking up with elements of Patton's US 3rd Army near Dijon and pressing eastwards down the Belfort Gap. It was now up to General Friedrich Wiese's 19th Army to bar the way to the encroaching enemy. Indeed, General Johannes Blaskowitz hoped and intended that Wiese should form a loose cordon that would permit the remaining elements of his depleted Army Group G to retreat safely northeastwards into the Belfort Gap.

The 11th Panzer Division rolled into Besançon on the evening of 5 September to cover the first units from the 19th Army moving into Belfort. Allied Intelligence intercepts showed that the 11th Panzer Division was hardly a viable rearguard; it now consisted of just nine panzers and six old French tanks, supported by five 88mm guns with 400 rounds between them. A month before, the 11th Panzer Division had fielded seventy-nine powerful Panther tanks, but just four days before reaching Besançon this number had fallen to just thirty, plus sixteen Panzer Mk IVs and four old Mk IIIs. The unit was subsequently strengthened by Panzer Brigade 113, which would have boosted the division's armoured strength with ten Panthers and three Mk IVs, thus providing it with a total of forty Panthers, nineteen Mk IVs and four Mk IIIs. Despite these welcome additions, the 11th Panzer Division's inventory was far below its authorised strength of ninety-one Panzer Mk IVs, seventy-nine Panthers and twenty-one StuG III assault guns.

Apart from the 11th Panzer Division, most of Wiese's combat forces were essentially improvised Kampfgruppen (battle groups) made up from the remnants of his infantry divisions and fleeing rear echelon units. To help bolster these, the German high command ordered the 30th Waffen-SS Division to France for anti-partisan duties. This unit arrived in Strasbourg on 18 August with instructions to hold the entrance to the Belfort Gap and counter any FFI units operating in the area.

General de Lattre's French 1st Corps was counterattacked west of Belfort along the Doubs river by German forces in the Montbeliard area on 8 September and the French were driven back. Also that day the German 1st Army returned to Blaskowitz's control and his command became a full army group once again. This, though, was simply a formality, as most of the units earmarked for Hitler's planned counterattack came from the 1st Army anyway.

The construction of German rear area defences, which were soon to become the front line, was the responsibility of local Nazi Party officials. It was not long before General Blaskowitz fell out with Gauleiter (District Leader) Adolf Wagner, who answered to SS-Reichsführer Heinrich Himmler. The Todt Organisation did not start work on the rear defences until September, by which time such efforts were largely too late. While the front-line troops doggedly fought delaying actions, little was achieved behind them despite their sacrifice.

Blaskowitz sent General Hans Taeglichsbeck to assess the situation between Nancy and Belfort. He found that even the strongpoints necessary for holding the mountain passes were only at the most preliminary stages. This was news that Blaskowitz did not want to hear. It also seemed that Himmler intended to take direct command of these defensive lines behind Blaskowitz, thereby hampering the operational chain of command. Blaskowitz's vocal protests understandably upset both Himmler and Wagner.

On 1 September the headquarters of the French 1st Corps was assembled at Aix to command troops as a subordinate corps of the French 1st Army. It was now under the command of the able Lieutenant-General Émile Béthouart, a veteran of both the 1940 campaign in Norway and the Allied landings in French North Africa in November 1942. The corps' main component divisions were colonial formations, consisting of the 2nd Moroccan Infantry Division, the 4th Moroccan Mountain Division, the 9th Colonial Infantry Division and the 1st Armoured Division. All these units had been forged in the fires of war.

In the south the French army also had two further divisions available. The French 2nd Armoured Division, formed on 1 May 1943, was redesignated the 5th Armoured Division on 16 July 1943 (thus allowing the 2nd Free French Division to convert to the 2nd Armoured) in North Africa. Originally comprising a tank brigade and a support brigade, the 5th Armoured Division was re-equipped and reorganized to American standards with three combat commands, which were detached to support French infantry divisions. The French 3rd Algerian Infantry Division was created in Algeria on 1 May 1943 from elements of the Constantine Division of the garrison of French North Africa. It moved to Italy in December 1943 and campaigned as far north as Siena as part of the French Expeditionary Corps, then withdrew to prepare for the landings in southern France.

The Allies' logistic situation was improving by early November, coinciding with orders from Eisenhower, now in charge of all Allied forces in northwestern Europe, calling for a broad offensive all along the entire French front. In the meantime the inactivity of the French 1st Corps misled Hitler into believing they were digging in for the winter and he reduced his forces in the Belfort Gap to a single understrength infantry division. Just before the Vosges campaign commenced, the German 198th Infantry Division was reinforced with men from six different battalions and five different regiments, including troops from two *Kriegsmarine* units. None of these did much to bolster the division's lamentable combat capabilities.

The French attacked the Belfort Gap on 13 November 1944. The German divisional commander was killed near the front lines; the commander of the 4th Luftwaffe Field Corps only narrowly escaped capture. Six days later French armour pushed through the Belfort Gap and reached the Rhine at Huningue. The defenders were dispersed in isolated pockets, particularly in Belfort itself, and troops of the 2nd Moroccan, 9th Colonial and 1st Armoured Divisions were able to move through the German lines.

General Thumm, commanding the German 64th Corps facing the US 6th Corps, issued an order of the day on 21 November exhorting his troops to fight

standing at the borders of our fatherland for the life of the people, of the soldiers' families, and of Germany herself. . . . The order to hold out to the last man must be executed under all circumstances . . . Great decisions are being made here and now. I expect all commanders, leaders and troops to hold out, not to lose their nerve, and fight to the last breath ... The decision falls on this side of the Rhine.

By 24 November the German 308th Grenadier-Regiment was trapped, its men forced either to surrender or to intern themselves in Switzerland. The following day the 1st Corps liberated Mulhouse, taken by a surprise armoured drive, and Belfort was assaulted by the Moroccans. General de Lattre, appreciating that the Germans were conducting an almost entirely static defence, directed both his corps to advance on Burnhaupt in the southern Vosges mountains to encircle the German 63rd Corps (formerly the 4th Luftwaffe Corps). By the 28th this operation had been completed, capturing more than 10,000 German troops and crippling the 63rd Corps. French losses were such that plans to clear the Alsatian Plain had to be shelved while both sides reorganised for the next round of bloodletting.

A heavily camouflaged Sherman tank, belonging to the French 5th Armoured Division supported by French commandos, engaging enemy targets on 20 November 1944 during the liberation of Belfort. This strategic city is located in the gap between the Vosges mountains to the north and the Jura mountains to the south.

French troops and Maquis fighters, armed with British weapons including a Sten gun and a Bren light machine gun, covering a major intersection in Belfort on 21 November 1944.

A French woman exhilarated by the liberation of Belfort on 25 November 1944. Actually Belfort had been liberated by the 1st French Corps three days earlier.

A knocked-out Jagdpanzer 38(t) Hetzer. This tank destroyer, armed with a 75mm PaK39 L/48, went into production in April 1944 and was issued to the tank-hunter detachments. Its small and compact design made it ideal for defensive operations.

Another Hetzer abandoned at the roadside. Note the ubiquitous 'Jerry' can dangling from the back of the vehicle. By this stage of the war, lack of fuel was often a problem.

This German tank destroyer is a Panzer IV/70(A) produced by Alkett. It was very similar in appearance to the Panzer IV/70(V) built by Vomag. Both variants were armed with a 75mm PaK42 L/70 gun mounted on a Panzer MK IV chassis, and both went into production in August 1944. Like the Hetzer, they were ideal defensive weapons. The French tanks encountered the Panzer IV/70(A).

The Wirbelwind was a much rarer type of flak panzer mounting the quad 20mm Flakvierling; the 20mm was much less effective than the 37mm gun on the Möbelwagen, and fewer than a hundred examples were built during 1944.

As the war dragged on, the Germans increasingly used their self-propelled flak guns in a ground-support role. The Möbelwagen was designed to give panzer units mobile anti-aircraft protection and consisted of a 37mm FlaK43 gun mounted on the basic Panzer IV hull. Protection for the crew was provided by a four-sided superstructure that could be lowered. Some 240 of these flak panzers were built by Deutsche-Eisenwerke from March 1944 onwards.

Forlorn-looking German troops captured by the French 1st Army in Alsace. In total, General Blaskowitz lost perhaps half of his 250,000 men in southern France.

Captured German equipment, including three Hetzers. More than 2,500 Hetzers were built. While the cramped fighting compartment was not popular with the crew, and the limited gun traverse caused problems, it was none the less a very successful tank destroyer.

Like the Hetzers in the previous shot, this one is sporting a three-tone camouflage scheme.

Yet more abandoned German armour (a Panzer Mk IV and a V) in the European Theatre of Operations. Hitler needlessly squandered his reserves trying to hold Lorraine.

Men of Patton's US 3rd Army who fought their way through Lorraine striking between Metz and Nancy in November 1944. Patton struggled to keep his army resupplied in the face of ever-changing Allied priorities.

Chapter Ten

Death in Colmar

After forcing the Belfort Gap, de Lattre's French 1st Army reached the Rhine in the region north of the Swiss border and south of the town of Colmar. In the meantime the French 2nd Armoured Division, spearheading the US 7th Army in the northern Vosges mountains, forced the Saverne Gap and also reached the Rhine, liberating Strasbourg. The net result of this was to compact the German presence in southern Alsace into a semicircular-shaped bridgehead that became known as the Colmar Pocket. This contained the exhausted German 19th Army. Forming the southern boundary was the French 1st Corps facing the Rhine at Huningue. It conducted an offensive in December to destroy the Colmar Pocket, but this operation was thwarted due to the requirement to cover more of the Allied front line as US units were shifted north in response to Hitler's surprise Ardennes offensive.

The latter half of November was a disaster for Hitler in Alsace. During the last two weeks of the month his forces facing the US 7th Army lost 17,500 men; 13,000 of them surrendered. Hungry, cold and demoralised, most of these men saw little point in resisting further. This left just 14,000 troops to fend off seven Allied divisions. However, the 7th Army's abrupt switch northwards not only robbed the Allies of the chance to take a short cut into the heart of Nazi Germany, but gave Hitler additional time to strengthen his West Wall defences along the Rhine. The weather also aided him, as Alsace during December is typically cloudy with ground fog and drizzle; Allied bombers had only five clear days to attack.

Hitler was determined to hold the Colmar Pocket and during the first half of December reinforced it with 8,000 men. (These men represented 80 per cent of the reinforcements sent to fight the US 6th Army Group.) His plan was to strike north through the French to attack the US 7th Army. The German 19th Army deployed nine divisions to try to halt French attempts at stopping the pocket from becoming a threat to liberated Strasbourg.

On 1 January 1945 Hitler launched Operation Nordwind, aimed at retaking Alsace. Only after the US 7th and French 1st Armies had held and turned back his offensive were they able to resume their efforts to reduce the troublesome Colmar Pocket.

There was no hiding that the pocket between Strasbourg and Mulhouse was an embarrassment to the Allies, especially to the French 1st Army which had singularly failed to make inroads into Hitler's last foothold on French soil. On 15 January the French were ordered to 'Launch without delay and by surprise, with all the means now at your disposal, powerful offensive operations converging in the direction of Brisach and aimed at the total reduction of the Alsace Bridgehead.' In reality, it was another week before they were in anything like a fit enough state to follow these orders.

On 20 January the French 1st Corps led the attack, but met stiff German resistance and the advance stalled as the German 19th Army fed in reinforcements. It would take three weeks for the French and the US 21st Corps to overwhelm the 19th Army, with the defenders putting up fierce resistance in extremely cold weather and fighting over ground that offered the attackers little or no cover. Notably General Émile Béthouart's 2nd and 4th Moroccan Divisions were assigned to take Ensisheim, with secondary attacks on the right flank of the corps north of Mulhouse carried out by the 9th Colonial Division. Armoured support was provided by the French 1st Armoured Division. Fighting in heavily wooded and urban areas meant that the terrain favoured the defenders.

Attacking in a snowstorm, the 1st Corps initially achieved tactical surprise against General Abraham's 63rd Army Corps. This attack forced General Siegfried Rasp to commit his only reserves, comprising Panzer Brigade 106, the 654th Heavy Anti-tank Battalion and the 2nd Mountain Division. In reality, Panzer Brigade 106 was not up to much as it had already been mauled in the fighting in Lorraine.

On the night of 20 January German counterattacks managed to halt the 1st Corps, and the Germans' in-depth defences, poor weather and exposed geography combined to hamper the French advance and limit its success. The German defences took a particular toll on French armour. The French 1st Armoured Division's Combat Command 1, for example, lost thirty-six of its fifty medium tanks to mines, and other tank units suffered similarly high casualties. It was evident that the Germans had no intention of giving up the fight.

While the French fought their way across the river Ill, American GIs from the 7th Infantry Division advanced into Ostheim on 23 January, despite unwelcome resistance from panzers. These were soon silenced by American bazooka teams and the town was secured. On the other side of the river American troops headed towards the Colmar Canal and were counterattacked by more panzers. Sherman tanks were called to their assistance, but the weight of the lead tank brought the bridge across the Ill crashing down. The isolated GIs fought on while bridging engineers struggled to span the river. At 2030 hours General John W. O'Daniel, commander of the US 3rd Division, ordered the 30th Infantry Regiment to 'Take over the attack with the same objectives . . . plan is now to hold the bridgehead and line along the Ill river. We will get the bridge that tank fell thru back in, send armour across and attack again.' It was completed at 0730 hours the next morning.

This time German 88mm anti-tank guns were waiting for them, with predictable results; minutes later panzers roared from the cover of the Riedwihr forest to attack the survivors. Across the Colmar Plain a desperate tank and artillery battle raged for the rest of the day, leaving numerous Shermans and Panzers flaming hulks. It was evident that the German 19th Army was far from defeated.

General de Monsabert's French 2nd Corps, with the US 3rd 'Rock of the Marne' Infantry Division and the French 1st March Infantry Division, launched its attack on 22/23 January. To the south of the 3rd Division, the US 28th 'Keystone' Infantry Division (whose battle honours included the liberation of Paris) held its sector of the front with the French 2nd Armoured Division in reserve. General O'Daniel's 3rd Infantry attacked to the southeast, aiming to cross the Ill river, bypass the city of Colmar to the north and open a path for the French 5th Armoured Division to cut the vital railway bridge at Neuf-Brisach, which was used to resupply the Germans in the Colmar Pocket.

In the face of this dogged German resistance, de Lattre signalled the US 6th Army Group for reinforcements. Its commander, General Devers, agreed and placed a corps headquarters at his disposal. General Milburn's 21st Corps moved into position between the two French Corps on 28 January, assuming control of three American infantry divisions and an armoured division. In addition, Milburn was placed in charge of three French formations: the 5th Armoured Division, the 1st Parachute Regiment and the 1st Commando Battalion.

Milburn was given the job of taking Colmar itself and reaching the bridge at Brisach. Elements of the US 21st Corps were instructed to take over part of the French sector and attack towards Neuf-Brisach to cut off the German escape route from Colmar. From the north the rest of the corps forced its way towards Colmar in the face of a bitter German rearguard action. Pressure from French and American forces was such that by the end of the month, Hitler was forced to redistribute his troops.

The 3rd Division continued its south and east sidestepping manoeuvre. German defences were deluged with hot metal. On the evening of 29 January divisional artillery fired 16,000 105mm and 155mm shells during a three-hour preparation for the assault of the 7th and 15th Infantry Regiments south across the Colmar canal. The infantry crossed between 2100 hours and midnight. After the crossings were secured, engineers began the construction of three Bailey bridges over the canal to enable armoured vehicles to cross. The following day the French armoured combat commands from the 5th Armoured Division crossed the canal to support the Americans.

The French 1st Parachute Regiment, deployed in the 3rd Division's area of responsibility, struggled to clear Widensolen on the 31st. Troops from the 3rd Division reached the Rhône–Rhine canal, 8km southeast of their crossing points over the Colmar canal, at 1700 hours that day. The French combat command supporting the Americans was given a brutal reception; with just thirteen tanks and thirty men in its rifle company remaining, it was taken out of the line and replaced by a unit from the French 2nd Armoured Division. On 1 February 1945 the 15th and 30th Infantry Divisions struck south along the Rhône–Rhine canal, reaching a point to the north of Neuf-Brisach. Over the next few days the 7th Infantry Division fought southwards along the same canal, passing through Artzenheim and taking Biesheim.

The 1st Corps struck again in early February, moving north to link up with the US 21st Corps at Rouffach, south of Colmar, after pushing through weak German resistance and reaching the bridge over the Rhine at Chalampé. On 4 February the 1st Corps attacked north across the Thur river; encountering only limited resistance, the 4th Moroccan Mountain Division drove to the southern outskirts of Rouffach. Abandoned by the Germans, Cernay was occupied the same day. Afterwards in Rouffach the Moroccans linked up with the US 12th Armored Division, and the 9th Colonial Infantry Division attacked Ensisheim. Hirtzfelden was taken by the 2nd Moroccan Infantry Division on 6 February and the 9th Colonial finished securing Ensisheim.

Shermans of the French 5th Armoured Division rumbled into Colmar on 2 February 1945 to a tumultuous reception from the population. This linking up of the 21st Corps and the French cut the pocket in two and enemy resistance quickly crumbled. Hitler finally abandoned his last foothold west of the Rhine when his men withdrew over the river and blew up the bridge at Chalampé.

Hitler's 19th Army lost up to 40,000 men, as well as 55 armoured vehicles and 66 artillery pieces. The German 2nd Mountain Division alone suffered 1,000 combat casualties and lost 4,700 men captured. Although the pocket was sealed by 9 February, the bulk of the 19th Army escaped over the Upper Rhine. Those remaining German forces in the French 1st Corps area retreated over the Rhine into Baden. From now on the thrust of the Allied offensive moved to the north, and the French were assigned the defence of the Rhine river from the area south of Strasbourg to the Swiss frontier until mid-April. The French victory at Colmar was complete and French honour avenged.

By late March Patch's US 7th Army in conjunction with Patton's push from the north had overrun the Saar-Palatinate triangle. The region was in chaos and the German 1st and 7th Armies had lost 100,000 prisoners in the space of two weeks. They had gone from controlling twenty-three divisions to losing 75 per cent of their combat effectives in one stroke. In the meantime the US 7th Army's zone west of the

Rhine had been cleared of German resistance. They crossed at Worms on 26 March 1945, allowing a breakout towards Darmstadt.

By early April the 19th Army was of little more than divisional strength, with about 10,500 combat effectives; now holding the Siegfried Line and the Black Forest, it was at risk of being outflanked. The German 1st Army was facing the US 6th and 21st Corps with just 7,500 troops. The German 7th Army, in even more dire straits with a combat strength of just 4,000, was also forced back by the US 3rd Army and the US 7th Army's 15th Corps.

With the end now in sight, the only real front line on the Western Front ran from the Löwenstein Hills to Nuremberg. This was held by a motley collection of 15,000 men supported by a hundred panzers and self-propelled guns and twenty battalions of artillery. On 22 April the Americans and the French 1st Army reached the Danube, which was followed by an attack on the city of Ulm.

The German 1st Army, under General Foertsch, could muster fewer than 500 combat effectives, supported by some 7,000 SS troops, by 1 May 1945. Likewise the 19th Army, commanded by General Erich Brandenberg, with a strength of just 3,000 men, did not have any divisions capable of effective defensive combat. The latter formally surrendered at 1500 hours on 5 May to the US 6th Corps and the French 1st Army. That day Foertsch also surrendered his command to the US 3rd Infantry Division. Ultimately the panzers in Lorraine had done nothing to stop the Americans' triumphal advance.

This American M10 Gun Motor Carriage has been whitewashed for the winter fighting. Armed with a 76.2mm (3in) gun mounted on the M4A2 Sherman chassis, it was one of the few Allied armoured fighting vehicles capable of taking on the panzers with any parity.

Likewise the M36 Gun Motor Carriage, which entered service in late 1944 and packed a mighty punch with its 90mm gun. This design utilised the M4A3 chassis fitted with the M36-type turret.

GIs moving forwards in their winter clothing. The fighting in the winter of 1944/5 was some of the toughest of the war.

German casualties. Hitler's Operation Northwind sought to recapture Alsace in order to keep the Allies away from the German border. Once this had been defeated, the French army sought to destroy the German bridgehead west of the Rhine based around the French city of Colmar.

French colonial divisions, including Moroccan troops, fought at Colmar. Three French armoured divisions supported them.

A heavy American mortar is used to pound German positions.

This German casualty was armed with the Stürmgewehr assault rifle.

US troops pushing forwards. Logistical problems greatly hampered their advance in the winter of 1944/5.

Shermans of the French 5th Armoured Division finally entered the city of Colmar on 2 February 1945, putting the Allies within striking distance of the Rhine.

Civilians cheer the liberating French army in Colmar. Their victory here marked the end of German occupation. Although the Colmar Pocket was sealed by 9 February 1945, the bulk of the German 19th Army managed to escape over the upper Rhine to fight another day.

German PoWs march into captivity under armed guard. The German defeat at Colmar cost Hitler upwards of 40,000 men and in the process his forces lost many of the survivors who had escaped from the Riviera.